ACTION SPORTS

SKATEBOARDING

Joe Herran and Ron Thomas

CHELSEA HOUSE
PUBLISHERS
A Haights Cross Communications Company
Philadelphia

This edition first published in 2003 in the United States of America by Chelsea House Publishers, a subsidiary of Haights Cross Communications.

Reprinted 2003

Chelsea House Publishers
1974 Sproul Road, Suite 400
Broomall, PA 19008-0914

The Chelsea House world wide web address is www.chelseahouse.com

Library of Congress Cataloging-in-Publication Data
Herran, Joe.
  Skateboarding / by Joe Herran and Ron Thomas.
    v. cm. — (Action sports)
  Includes index.
  Contents: What is skateboarding? — Skateboarding gear — Skateboarding safely — Making a skateboard — Maintaining the skateboard — Skills, tricks, and techniques — The skateboarding scene — Skateboarding champions — Girls and skateboarding — In competition —Then and now — Related action sports.
  ISBN 0-7910-6998-2
  1. Skateboarding—Juvenile literature. [1. Skateboarding.] I. Thomas, Ron, 1947- II. Title. III. Action sports (Chelsea House Publishers)
  GV859.8 .H45 2003

  796.22—dc21

                                                                                    2002002295

First published in 2002 by
MACMILLAN EDUCATION AUSTRALIA PTY LTD
627 Chapel Street, South Yarra, Australia, 3141

Edited by Miriana Dasovic
Text design by Karen Young
Cover design by Karen Young
Illustrations by Nives Porcellato and Andy Craig
Page layout by Raul Diche
Photo research by Legend Images

Printed in China

Acknowledgements
The authors wish to acknowledge and thank Greig Innes for his assistance and advice in the writing of this text.

Cover photo: Skateboarder, courtesy of Sport the library.

AAP/AP Photo/Paul Conners, p. 29 (right); AAP/AP Photo/Las Vegas Sun, Lori Cain, p. 21 (bottom right); AAP Image/Paul Rennell, p. 11 (top); Australian Picture Library/Corbis, pp. 12, 17 (top), 24 (left); Bill Bachman, pp. 6–7, 22 (top); Burton p. 30 (top); Coo-ee Picture Library, p. 19 (top); Getty Images/Hulton, pp. 28 (right), 29 (left); Legend Images, pp. 10–11, 13, 18, 22 (bottom); National Museum of Roller Skating, Lincoln, Nebraska, p. 28 (top left and bottom left); http://sirdna.com/skaters/elissa_steamer/imgs.html, p. 26; Sporting Images, pp. 19 (bottom), 20 (bottom); Sport the library, pp. 4, 5, 8–9, 15 (right), 16, 17 (bottom), 20 (top), 21 (top and bottom left), 23 (left and right), 24–25, 25 (right), 27, 30 (center and bottom).

CONTENTS

Introduction   4

What is skateboarding?   5

Skateboarding gear   6

Skateboarding safely   10

Making a skateboard   12

Maintaining the skateboard   13

Skills, tricks and techniques   14

The skateboarding scene   22

Skateboarding champions   23

Girls and skateboarding   26

In competition   27

Then and now   28

Related action sports   30

Glossary   31

Index   32

FEB 23 2004

INTRODUCTION

In this book you will read about:

- skateboards and how they are made
- the gear used by skateboarders
- the safety measures used to keep skateboarders safe
- the basic skills of skateboarding

- tricks and stunts performed by experienced and professional riders on the streets or in the halfpipe
- some of the top skateboarders in competition today
- the history of the sport from its beginnings in the 1940s.

In the beginning

Skateboarding began in the late 1940s. Scooters were popular then, but expensive. Some kids who could not afford scooters took the wheels off their roller skates and attached them to a piece of wood. They nailed a handle to this new vehicle. Later, they decided to remove the handle and ride on just the wooden platform. Soon after, some surfers began to ride on skateboards. The first true skateboards, with clay wheels, were commercially made and sold in the 1950s.

Skateboarding today

Skateboarding is now a popular sport in countries throughout the world. Competitions attracting hundreds of professional and **amateur** competitors, of both sexes, are held in countries around the world. **Skate parks** have been built in cities and towns everywhere. Skateboard design is improving all the time. Special shoes and clothing have been designed and made for skateboarders. Extreme sports (X Games) featuring skateboarding draw huge crowds.

⬊ Warning This is not a how-to book for aspiring skateboarders. It is intended as an introduction to the exciting world of skateboarding and a look at where the sport has come from and where it is heading.

WHAT IS SKATEBOARDING?

There are two types of skateboarding: street and vert.

Street skateboarding

Street skateboarding is done anywhere but on a ramp. Tricks are performed on streets and roads, in car parks and school grounds – wherever the surface is flat and safe. Skate parks are an ideal venue for all kinds of skateboarding. They have super-smooth surfaces as well as ramps, stairs, curbs and **funboxes**. Street skateboarders jump, flip and **grind** over and on all kinds of surfaces and objects. Street skateboarding also includes skateboard racing.

Skateboard racing

Riders push off from a starting position, then race one another down a winding and sloping piece of roadway. They stand or kneel on the fast-moving skateboard and can reach speeds of 40 miles (65 kilometers) per hour and more.

Vert skateboarding

Vert (short for vertical) skateboarding is done on the halfpipe. This is a huge U-shaped ramp between $11\frac{1}{2}$ and $14\frac{3}{4}$ feet (3.5 and 4.5 meters) high. It has a flat surface of approximately $16\frac{1}{2}$ feet (5 meters) at the bottom, called the flatbottom. There are also quarter-pipe ramps. Vert skateboarders jump, flip and grind in the halfpipe.

STREET

VERT

5

SKATEBOARDING GEAR

The board

The skateboard has three parts:

- deck
- wheels
- trucks.

Deck

The board the skateboarder stands on is called the deck. The shape of the board is concave or dish-like, with the nose and tail curved upward to make it easier for the skateboarder to stay on the board. An extra length at the front of the board is called the front kick or nose, and the extra length at the end of the board is the back kick or tail. The front kick and back kick help skaters do more complex tricks. When a skateboarder pushes down on the back kick, the front of the board rises slightly off the ground. This makes the board easier to steer and **maneuver** while doing tricks.

Most decks are between 7 and $8\frac{1}{2}$ inches (18 and 22 centimeters) wide, and 31 and 33 inches (79 and 84 centimeters) long. They come in various widths. Wider decks are used for street skating, and narrower skateboards are used for freestyle skating and jumping.

Wheels

Wheels are made of urethane. This is a tough, springy plastic that can be made in different sizes and hardnesses. Smaller wheels, with diameters of between 50 and 56 millimeters, are light and good for street skating. Wheels with diameters of between 58 and 65 millimeters are heavier.

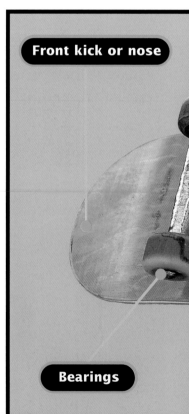

Front kick or nose

Bearings

These are perfect for skating on rough, cracked concrete. Professional vert skaters often use large-diameter wheels as they make for a faster ride. Softer wheels give a smoother ride, while hard wheels help the rider snap the tail off the ground and jump higher into the air.

Bearings

Bearings are found inside the wheels. They are important because they keep the wheels turning properly. The bearings are precision-made by machines from high-quality steel.

Trucks

The trucks help the skateboarder steer and control the skateboard. Trucks are made of cast aluminum or titanium and support the wheels. There are two trucks on a skateboard. Each truck consists of a hanger with an axle inside it, a rubber cushion to aid steering, and a kingpin to keep the truck stable. A baseplate attaches the trucks to the bottom of the deck. The wheels are bolted onto the trucks.

The more loosely the trucks are fitted to the deck, the easier it is to make a turn on a skateboard. Trucks have to be very strong to allow the skateboarder to do various tricks, but they also need to be light, reliable and maneuverable.

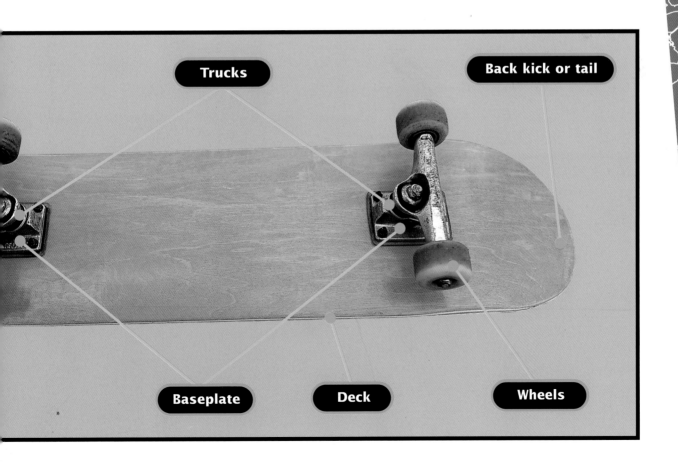

Trucks

Back kick or tail

Baseplate

Deck

Wheels

Other gear

A skateboarder needs protection for the head, knees, elbows, wrists and hands. A helmet, wrist guards, gloves, and knee and elbow pads are essential pieces of equipment, especially for beginner skateboarders and those doing high-powered tricks in the halfpipe. Safety gear allows daredevil skateboarders to try more difficult tricks without having to worry about serious injuries.

Shoes

The first skateboarders skated in bare feet! Injuries soon made skateboarders realize that they needed protection from scrapes, cuts and burns. Sneakers that were strong, flexible and capable of gripping the skateboard were needed. Most of the big sporting-shoe companies now make slip-resistant shoes for skateboarders. The shoes have become very fashionable and are even worn by people who do not skateboard. Good skateboarding shoes should cushion the skater's feet and be very durable.

Helmets

The helmet should be made of light plastic and be padded on the inside. It should fit well without being too tight. A skateboarder wearing a correctly fitting helmet is safe, comfortable and can see and hear clearly.

Gloves and wrist guards

Wrist guards have hard plastic splints inside them to prevent the wrists from bending the wrong way. Gloves are worn to protect the hands from cuts and grazes.

Padding

Plastic caps on knee and elbow pads help to absorb the shock to the body when a skateboarder falls. The hardened caps have proven to be perfect for **sliding** down the surfaces of ramps. Skateboarders are able to escape serious injury by sliding onto their knee pads.

Clothes

Clothes should be loose and comfortable to allow for plenty of movement. Padded shorts are also available to protect a skater's hips and seat. The pads can be bought separately and worn inside the skater's own shorts.

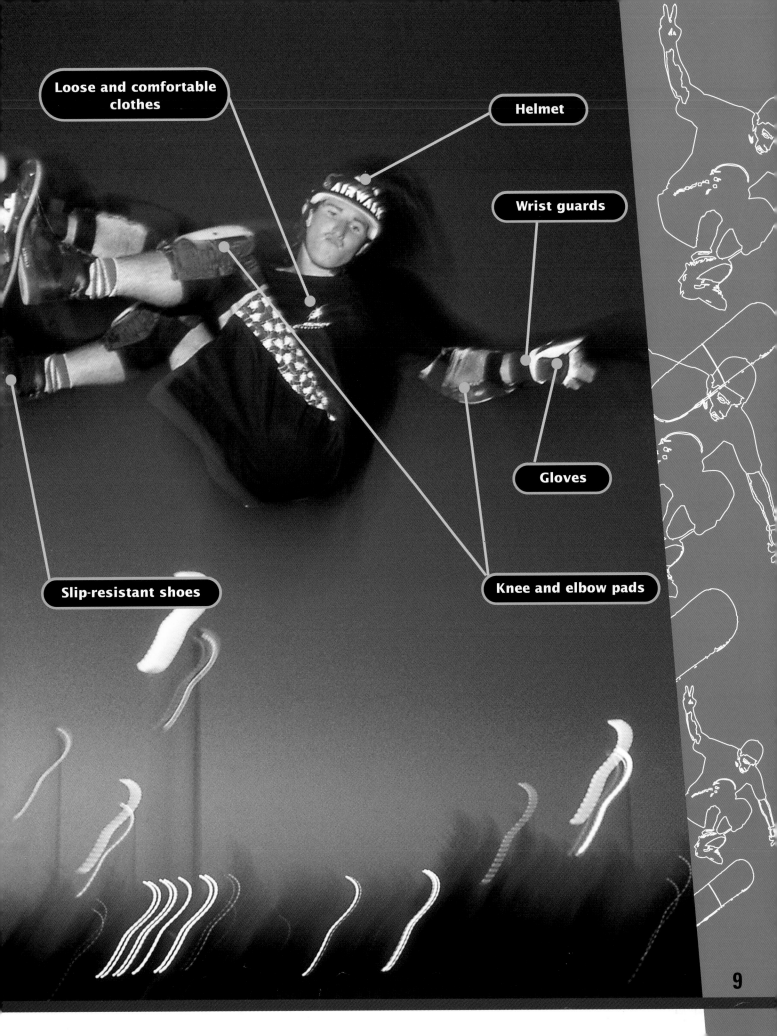

Loose and comfortable clothes

Helmet

Wrist guards

Gloves

Slip-resistant shoes

Knee and elbow pads

SKATEBOARDING
SAFELY

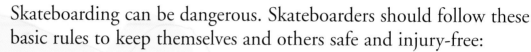

Skateboarding can be dangerous. Skateboarders should follow these basic rules to keep themselves and others safe and injury-free:

- choose flat, safe ground on which to learn the basic skills of speed control, turning and stopping
- skate in control at all times
- wear protective gear, helmet, wrist guards, knee and elbow pads
- wear light-colored clothing, reflective strips on their wrist pads, and have a skate light fitted to the back of the boot shell and to the helmet when skateboarding at night or in dull conditions
- give way to pedestrians
- practice carefully before attempting new tricks
- skate with friends, in case of accidents
- skate in a safe place and keep out of traffic
- let other skateboarders know what they are doing
- wait their turn when using skate parks
- keep the skateboard and protective gear in good working order
- watch out for road hazards.

Falling safely

Learning how to fall is a skill that all skateboarders need. When a skateboarder is losing balance, they should crouch down so that they have a shorter distance to fall. If the rider does fall, it is best to land on fleshy parts of the body and to try to roll during the fall. Trying to stop a fall with the arms can mean broken bones!

Skateboarders should learn bailing. This is kicking the board away when a trick goes wrong. By bailing, the falling skateboarder does not land on the skateboard.

Learning to knee-slide is a good idea for all skateboarders doing tricks. Riders fall onto their knee pads and slide out of danger when a trick goes wrong.

↗ To bail on a ramp, the skater steps off the board and slides down the **transition** on kneepads.

GETTING READY TO RIDE

↙ Gentle stretching, jogging or jumping will warm up and loosen muscles before taking to the skateboard. Warm, loose muscles work better and are less likely to cramp or suffer sprains and torn ligaments.

MAKING A SKATEBOARD

The deck

The deck on the first skateboards was a solid piece of wood such as oak or maple. These hardwood boards were heavy and stiff. Over the years, skateboard manufacturers experimented with all kinds of materials for the decks. Fiberglass, aluminum and even molded plastic were tried, but most boards today are made of wood, usually maple. About seven thin layers of maple are pressed tightly and glued together under pressure. This laminating gives the board great flexibility, helping the skateboarder to do many tricks.

The tail, nose and concave bends are molded by machine. Once they are shaped, the decks are cut out on a jigsaw, sanded smooth and sprayed with varnish. Holes are then drilled to a pre-set size for the trucks. The top of the deck is covered with grip tape. This is a sticky-backed material that resembles sandpaper. The rough surface of the grip tape makes it easier for the soles of the skateboarder's shoes to grip the board. There is usually a striking graphic or picture on the bottom of the deck.

↘ Signature decks are made and sold to fans around the world.

Signature decks

Many top professional skateboarders have their own signature decks. These are signed by the skateboarder and have a graphic design that is unique to them.

MAINTAINING THE
SKATEBOARD

A skateboard needs little maintenance. Skateboarders need to:

- wipe the bearings clean occasionally so the wheels can spin quickly and smoothly
- check the screws on the truck mountings and keep them tight
- check the trucks for cracks and replace any cracked truck
- check the alignment of the trucks so that the board will ride straight
- replace the cushions occasionally
- replace the pivot rubber
- check for **delaminations** or splits in the nose and tail, and glue them if necessary
- clean off mud and dirt on the grip tape to keep the surface rough
- rotate the wheels to make sure they wear evenly.

 The screws on the truck mounting should be checked and tightened if necessary.

THE SKATEBOARDER'S TOOL

A skate wrench is a multipurpose tool carried by skateboarders for tightening trucks and carrying out other minor adjustments to the skateboard.

SKILLS, TRICKS AND
TECHNIQUES

The basics

Standing on the board

The first thing a skateboarder learns is how to stand on the board. There are two positions: regular foot and goofy foot. The correct position is the one that feels most comfortable. Professional skateboarders master switch stance, which means they can ride both regular and goofy.

REGULAR FOOT

The left foot is forward and pointed toward the front of the board, with the right foot behind.

GOOFY FOOT

The right foot is forward and pointed toward the front of the board, with the left foot behind.

Turning (carving)

With the knees slightly bent, the skateboarder leans in the direction of the turn. The trucks do the rest. There are two basic turns:

- the frontside turn – where the skateboarder faces the direction of the turn and leans toward the toes
- the backside turn – where the skateboarder leans back a little on the heels and turns the board with their back to the turn.

Stopping

There are several ways to stop the skateboard:

- jumping off the skateboard
- dragging the back foot on the ground until the board eventually stops
- taking the back foot off the board and using it to run forward, gradually slowing to a stop. This is faster than dragging the foot.

PUSHING

 To start the skateboard, the skater pushes hard against the ground with the back foot and is propelled forward, like riding a scooter. The skateboarder rolls along and, when ready, places both feet on the board.

CARVING

 Turns can be done either frontside or backside.

Beyond the basics

The ollie

Most skateboarding tricks are based on just one move, the ollie. This trick was made famous by Alan 'Ollie' Gelfand in the mid-1970s. During an ollie, a skateboarder leaps into the air with the board seemingly glued to his or her feet. The ollie is used to jump over just about anything.

To perform an ollie, the skateboarder stands on the board with the back foot on the tail and the front foot in the middle of the deck. The skateboarder crouches down with the hands almost touching the ground. Then the skateboarder **pops the tail**, slides the front foot toward the nose and lifts the back foot. Rider and board are now airborne, and the rider's knees are tucked into the chest. The skateboarder levels out the board by sliding the shoes across the grip tape toward the nose before landing with knees bent and riding off.

An ollie is snappy but smooth. It takes practice but has to be learned before a skateboarder can do other tricks.

180 turn

With both feet on the stationary skateboard, the rider leans back so that the front of the board lifts into the air. At the same time, the rider pivots on the back foot to turn the skateboard. Experienced skateboarders can turn 180 degrees (half a circle) or even 360 degrees (a complete circle).

 This beginner skateboarder practices the 180 turn.

Acid drop

The acid drop involves riding a skateboard off a small drop such as a street curb. The skateboarder skates directly toward the edge of the curb and leans back so that the front wheels lift into the air. The skateboard rolls over the curb on the back wheels. The front wheels come down, then the skater absorbs the landing by shifting their weight to the center of the board before skating away.

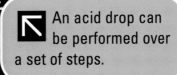 An acid drop can be performed over a set of steps.

Street skating tricks

Most street skating tricks are done off street curbs, down stairs or over other drops.

50-50

The skateboarder approaches the curb at a moderate to fast speed. Just before the skateboard hits the curb, the rider rolls the board **parallel** to the curb and ollies. After landing back on the board, the skateboarder grinds or rides along the edge of the curb on the trucks.

50-50

Shuv-its

The skateboarder's back foot is in position for an ollie, while the front foot is between the middle of the board and the front screws. The skater gives the board a pop, then shoves it around with the front foot. This makes the board turn 180 degrees beneath the skateboarder's feet. The skater lands back on the board after it has spun and rides off.

SHUV-IT

↗ The skater pops the board in preparation for the shove that will turn it 180 degrees.

Kickflip

The skateboarder crouches down and then starts to lift as if doing an ollie. The rider then pushes down on the tail with the back foot and kicks the front foot up and out. The board flips over and, when the board is right side up, the rider lands in a crouched position.

Grinds and slides

Skateboarders slide along street curbs, rails and steps on one or both trucks. The faster the rider is moving, the longer the grind will last. There are different types of slides:

- tailslide – sliding on the tail
- noseslide – sliding on the nose
- boardslide – sliding on the middle of the board.

KICKFLIP

TAILSLIDE

Tricks on the vert ramp or halfpipe

Pumping

Vert ramps are giant U-shaped ramps more than 13 feet (4 meters) long. To begin skateboarding on a ramp, the skateboarder starts on the flatbottom and rides up and down the ramp a little. As the skateboarder begins to feel comfortable with this, they start using their weight to push against the curve of the ramp. This is called pumping, and causes the skateboard to gain speed and momentum.

Kickturns

Once the skater is pumping up and down with ease, the next thing to try are kickturns. When reaching the top of the ramp, the skateboarder stays crouched down and kicks the back of the skateboard to lift the front wheel. The rider then rotates and spins on the back wheels to turn the board 180 degrees.

Drop-in

To drop-in, the skateboarder starts at the top of the ramp. The tail of the skateboard sits on the platform at the top of the ramp and the rest hangs over the **coping**. With the back foot on the tail and the front foot over the front truck, the skater crouches down and leans forward. When all the skater's weight is over the coping, the skater pushes down with the front foot. The wheels hit the ramp and the skater rides away to the flatbottom.

180-DEGREE KICKTURN

DROP-IN

20

Fakie nosestall or tailstall

The skateboarder pumps on the halfpipe until reaching the top of the ramp. While going **fakie** toward the other side, the skateboarder gets ready to press down on the nose. This is done when the skateboarder reaches the top, where the rider presses down so that the nose goes on to the coping of the halfpipe. The rider stalls (stops) for a bit, then drops-in again.

Ollie grab

The skater grabs the skateboard with one hand at the highest point of the jump. The grab helps the rider control the board in midair and turn more easily.

FAKIE TAILSTALL

OLLIE GRAB

ACTION FACT

A famous professional skateboarder, Danny Way, once jumped out of a helicopter to drop-in on a ramp about 10 feet (3 meters) below before riding away.

DANNY WAY'S JUMP

21

THE SKATEBOARDING
SCENE

Skateboarding around the world

Even in countries outside the United States, such as Australia, skateboarding has become a popular sport for young people. Skateboarding in the city streets can be dangerous for both skaters and pedestrians, so skateboarding parks have been built in cities and towns around the world. Skateboarding is a fun way for young people to exercise and enjoy themselves.

Finding out more about skateboarding

There are many books and magazines about skateboarding. The internet has many sites about the sport, and there are videos showing top skateboarders in action. Programs on TV about extreme sports also feature skateboarding.

↗ Skate parks are safe places for skateboarding.

↘ Skateboarding magazines contain tricks and techniques and information about skateboarders.

Top skateboarders come from countries around the world, including Rune Glifberg from Denmark, Max Dufour and Geoff Rowley from Canada, Bob Burnquist from Brazil, and Andy Macdonald and Tony Hawk from the United States. Tas and Ben Pappas are Australian brothers who skateboard professionally and participate in competitions around the world.

SKATEBOARDING
CHAMPIONS

↗ Tas Pappas

- Born in 1975
- Lives in Melbourne, Australia
- Skates goofy foot
- Started competing in the mid-1990s

Career highlights

- First place in the vert competition in 1996 in Hollywood, California
- First place in the vert competition in 1999 at the B3 event in Portland, Oregon
- In Hollywood in 1996, Tas upset Tony Hawk, probably the most famous of all vert skateboarders, when he beat the champ to take first place.
- Involved in the Summer X Games since 1995 and has appeared in several skateboarding videos
- In 2000 and 2001, was among the top place-getters at the X Games in Melbourne, Australia and in Cleveland, Ohio, and at the Gravity Games in Providence, Rhode Island

↗ Ben Pappas

- Born in 1978
- Lives in Melbourne, Australia
- Skates regular foot

Career highlights

- In 1996, second place in the World Vert Competition
- One of his best results so far has been in the B3 competition in Oceanside, California in 1998 where he was placed 13th
- In 2000, fourth place at the X Games in Melbourne, Australia

↗ Tony Hawk

Tony Hawk is the most famous of all vert skateboarders. Tony started skateboarding with his brother at age nine. By the time he was 12, he was winning all the local skateboard contests.

- Born April 12, 1968 in San Diego
- Turned professional at the age of 14

Career highlights

- Has won nearly every vert title since his first win in 1982
- Has won more skate contests than any other skateboarder
- Was number one skateboarder in the National Skateboard Association Series in the United States for 11 years
- Has a computer game named after him
- Won seven X Games gold medals
- Was the first person to pull a '720' (two full-circle spins)
- Was the first skateboarder to complete a '900' in competition at the X Games in 1999. (A '900' is $2\frac{1}{2}$ turns at the top of the ramp)
- Was the first person to receive the Action Sports Achievement Award, an award first made in 2001
- Has performed stunts for TV commercials and in Hollywood movies. Practices skateboarding for two to three hours a day, five days a week
- Has started companies making skateboards and skateboard clothing
- In 2001: the Tony Hawk Tour. Tony and five other top skateboarders toured Europe and North America, giving exhibitions of skateboarding tricks

TONY HAWK IN ACTION

Tony has invented more than
50 tricks and maneuvers.

GIRLS AND SKATEBOARDING

AllGirl Skate Jam

Since it began, skateboarding has been an activity mainly for boys and young men. But in 1990, a skateboarding contest specifically for girls and young women was held in the United States. To give female skateboarders recognition, the AllGirl Skate Jam, an event for female skateboarders, was held in 1997. The AllGirl Skate Jam became an annual event in the United States, and in 2000 it became an international tour. Competitions took place in the United States, Spain and Brazil. In January 2001, there was an AllGirl Skate Jam competition in Australia.

Events included mini-ramp and halfpipe competitions as well as a jam-format street competition. In a jam, four or five girls skate at the same time for a set period of time. Both professional and amateur skateboarders compete.

Meet Elissa Steamer

Elissa Steamer has become one of the most famous female professional skateboarders. She was born in Fort Myers, Florida and now lives in California. Elissa has been skateboarding professionally since April 1998. She has made several videos demonstrating how to perform tricks on a skateboard. As well as competing against other female skateboarders, Elissa has competed against male skateboarders and has placed very highly in competitions.

ELISSA STEAMER

26

IN COMPETITION

Competitions today

Some of the biggest skateboarding competitions are the World Cup, held in Munster, Germany, and the Extreme or X Games, hosted by the ESPN sports network. The X Games feature skateboarding as well as several other 'extreme' sports such as in-line skating and BMX riding. As these events became more popular, they became more highly organized. New rules and strict codes for judging professional and amateur skateboarders were developed.

Judging

In professional competitions, there are usually five judges who must be experts in skateboarding. In vert skateboarding contests, some moves are compulsory, but skateboarders may add other tricks. The skateboarder tries to do as many different tricks as possible in about 45 seconds, using all parts of the ramp area. Judges give scores for:

- the difficulty of the moves made
- the variety of tricks
- how high a skateboarder jumps
- style (how the rider looks)
- linkage (how well the tricks follow each other).

THE EXTREME GAMES

THEN AND NOW

1700s	1863	1940s	Late 1950s	1960s
A Belgian called Joseph Merlin invented the first roller skates. Merlin was a well-known maker of musical instruments and other mechanical inventions. One of the first public showings of his invention was at a fancy dress party in London. Merlin lost control of the skates, crashed into the furniture and broke a mirror!	James Leonard Plimpton invented the first modern roller skates. These allowed skaters to turn instead of skating only in a straight line. Plimpton's design is still in use today.	Some kids who could not afford scooters made their own scooters without handles, creating the early skateboard.	The first true skateboards were commercially made and sold by a company called Roller Derby. The wheels used were made of clay instead of metal.	Skateboarding became a popular sport for surfers, and the first skateboarding competition was held in the United States.

1819

1863

1940s

1965	1973	1976	1978	1980	1990s
An International Skateboard Championship took place in Anaheim, California, and was shown on television.	Skateboarding became safer with the invention of urethane wheels by Frank Nasworthy. The addition of a kicktail to the deck and wider trucks made the skateboards easier to control. The first skateboarding moves copied the moves of surfing. The hang ten, carving, cut backs, walking the nose, and the coffin were all surfboard moves that skateboarders used.	The first outdoor skate park was built in Florida.	Alan Gelfand, one of the most famous skateboarders of the 1970s, invented the ollie. Other skateboarders soon developed their own moves.	Skateboard design was improved with the use of laminated 7-ply maple decks. Many of the tricks that were invented in the 1970s were improved upon during the 1980s. The sport became a part of punk and new wave music movements.	Skateboarding gained a great deal of exposure at the ESPN 2 Extreme Games and became the sixth-largest participant sport in the United States. Professional skateboarders toured the world, making a living from competition prize money and their endorsement deals with skateboard manufacturers.

1973

1990s

29

RELATED ACTION
SPORTS

Skateboarding in its earliest form has been around since the 1940s, but the first skate parks were not built until the 1970s. Skateboarding was the first aggressive or extreme sport. The following sports have developed from skateboarding, using many of the same moves and skills.

SNOWBOARDING

Snowboarding

Snowboarders glide over the snow with feet strapped to a board. Like skateboarders, snowboarders perform tricks and jumps on flat ground and slide along rails. In the halfpipe, they perform many of the same moves used by skateboarders. Snowboarders also race and slalom down mountain slopes.

IN-LINE SKATING

In-line skating

Like skateboarding, in-line skating is done for fun on streets and roads and in skate parks. Aggressive forms of the sport include jumping obstacles, and grinding and vert skating on the vert ramp or halfpipe. Many of the tricks and moves come from skateboarding.

AGGRESSIVE BMX

Aggressive BMX

Airs and other tricks performed in the halfpipe by skateboarders have been copied or adapted by vert BMX riders on the ramp.

GLOSSARY

airs tricks performed while the skateboarder is airborne

amateur an athlete who has never competed for money

coping the metal bar on a ramp used by the skateboarder to grind and slide

delaminations damage done to the laminate on a skateboard

fakie moving backwards

funbox a ramp in a skate park that has many sides, a launch ramp leading up to the deck, and a landing ramp on the opposite side

grind to ride along the coping of a ramp, or any other edge, on the trucks of the skateboard

maneuver to move skilfully

parallel running in the same direction while staying a fixed distance from something, such as a curb

pop the tail to slam down on the tail of the skateboard

skate park a specially designed and built venue for skateboarding

sliding the most commonly used method of stopping on a skateboard

transition the curved part of a skateboarding ramp

INDEX

A
acid drop 17
aggressive BMX 30
AllGirl Skate Jam 26

B
bearings 7

C
clothes 8
competition 4, 27

D
deck 6, 12
drop-in 20

F
fakie nosestall 21
falling 10–11
50-50 18

G
Gelfand, Alan 'Ollie'
   16, 29
grabs 21
grinds 19

H
halfpipe 5, 20
Hawk, Tony 23,
   24–5
helmets 8
history 4, 28–9

I
in-line skating 30

J
judging 27

K
kickflip 19
kickturns 20

M
Macdonald, Andy 19
Merlin, Joseph 28

O
ollie 16, 21
180 turn 17

P
Pappas, Ben 23
Pappas, Tas 23
Plimpton, James
   Leonard 28
pumping 20
pushing 15

S
safety 8, 10–11
shuv-its 18
signature decks 12
skateboard
   construction 12
skateboard
   maintenance 13

skateboard racing 5
skateboards 6–7, 12
skills 14–21
snowboarding 30
stance 14
Steamer, Elissa 26
stopping 15
street skateboarding
   5, 18–19

T
tailstall 21
tools 13
tricks 16–21
trucks 7
turning 15

V
vert skateboarding 5,
   20–1

W
Wainwright, Danny
   16
Way, Danny 21
wheels 6, 28

X
X Games 4, 27